The Kindness of Growing Together

By Kathy Grubb

Dedication

To every child who chooses kindness.

Introduction

This story is about friendship, teamwork, and how a small act of kindness can blossom into something beautiful. We hope it inspires you to start your own Kindness Patch!

Chapter 1: A New Term Begins

It was the first week back after the holidays, and the children at Willowbank Primary were still getting used to their new classroom. Something felt different this year—brighter, warmer. At the front of the room stood Miss Rose, their new teacher. She was young, energetic, and wore sunflower earrings that sparkled in the light.

On Friday morning, Miss Rose clapped her hands. "We're going outside," she said. "I have something exciting to show you." The class lined up curiously and followed her to a weedy patch behind the playground.

"This," she said, "will be our Kindness Patch."

No one spoke. Was this some punishment?

But Miss Rose continued, "We're going to grow things here—plants, flowers, vegetables, and kindness. You'll see."

Chapter 2: Big Ideas

Back in class, the children couldn't stop talking. They sketched garden ideas during free time—sunflowers, carrots, strawberries, and even pumpkins. Olivia suggested a friendship bench. Leo wanted to build a bug hotel. Someone else suggested herbs for the school kitchen.

Miss Rose made a list of all their ideas and promised they'd vote on what to start with.

They named it officially: "The Kindness Patch." And Nina and a few others got started on painting the wooden sign.

Chapter 3: Teamwork Begins

The next morning, the class gathered by the patch with gloves, trowels, and watering cans. Leo brought seeds from his grandad's allotment, and Olivia brought paint for the kindness sign.

They dug, weeded, and laughed. Tariq helped Leo loosen the soil, and Nina shared her snack with Grace. For the first time, everyone found a way to be involved.

By the end of the day, the patch was cleared and ready. Miss Rose smiled. "Teamwork is our first seed. Let's water it with kindness."

Chapter 4: Tiny Sprouts

Days turned into weeks. Little green shoots began to poke through the soil. The children checked them every morning. They kept journals and took turns watering the patch.

One day, Olivia noticed a single flower blooming near the edge. She called the others over. "Look!" she shouted. "It's started!"

Miss Rose gathered them into a circle. "Kindness is like gardening," she said. "You care for it every day—and one day, it blossoms."

They added new kindness notes to their classroom board.

Chapter 5: Giving Day

With the garden now blooming, Miss Rose announced a special idea. "Let's hold a Giving Day," she said. "A day where we give from our Kindness Patch."

The children prepared baskets of vegetables, herbs, and flowers. They made cards and wrapped bunches of lavender with ribbon. Parents and teachers were invited to visit.

On the day, the children gave away everything they had grown. Even Leo, who loved his sunflowers, handed one to the dinner lady.

"It's not about what we keep," Miss Rose said. "It's about what we give."

Chapter 6: Sharing Kindness

After Giving Day, the class began noticing small acts of kindness everywhere. Someone helped tidy the book corner. Another gave up their seat for a friend.

Inspired, they created a Kindness Tree in the corridor. Every time someone saw a kind act, they wrote it on a leaf and added it to the tree.

One day, the headteacher stopped by and smiled. "Your garden isn't just growing vegetables," he said. "It's growing kindness in the whole school."

Chapter 7: Growing at Home

Children began bringing stories back to class, not about school, but about their homes. Nina and her mum planted herbs in old teacups. Leo taught his little brother how to sow sunflower seeds.

Miss Rose created a new board in class: 'Growing at Home'. The board was filled with photos, drawings, and short notes.

Soon, parents started asking how to make their own Kindness Patch. The garden had grown far beyond the playground.

Chapter 8: New Shoots

The class got a letter from another school that had heard about the Kindness Patch. "Can you tell us how to start our own?" it said.

Miss Rose helped the class write back. They included drawings, tips, and even seed packets.

"They're planting kindness, too," Olivia said.

"Kindness is catching," added Leo.

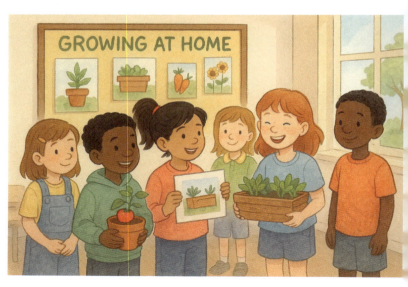

Chapter 9: All Are Welcome

One Monday morning, a new student named Tariq joined the class. He was quiet and held a small brown envelope tightly.

When it was time to visit the patch, he opened the envelope and showed seeds from his grandmother's garden. "She said they grow strong and tall."

The children made space and helped Tariq plant his seeds. They added a new painted sign: 'All Are Welcome Here'.

Chapter 10: A Patch of Kindness

As the school year drew to a close, the Kindness Patch was buzzing with bees and butterflies. Flowers bloomed in every colour.

On the last day, Miss Rose handed each child a small envelope with seeds and a journal titled 'My Kindness Patch'. "Plant these wherever you go," she said.

The children looked at their patch, now a beautiful mess of colour and life. They knew it wasn't the end.

It was only the beginning.

Kindness Moments I'll Remember

_____

_____

_____

_____

_____

_____

_____

_____

_____

_____

_____

_____

_____

_____

Our Garden Friendships

_____

_____

_____

_____

_____

_____

_____

_____

_____

_____

_____

_____

_____

_____

What Friendship Means to Me

What I'd Like to Grow Next Season

_____

_____

_____

_____

_____

_____

_____

_____

_____

_____

_____

_____

_____

_____

My Growing Space – At Home

_____

_____

_____

_____

_____

_____

_____

_____

_____

_____

_____

_____

_____

_____

My Growing Space – At School or Community

About the Author

Kathy Grubb is a community-focused writer who created this story to help children grow kindness, confidence, and connection. Through her work with ThriveTogetherCommunity.net, she supports schools and charities with tools that build hope and resilience.

Thank You

We hope your Kindness Patch grows strong and full of joy!

Printed in Dunstable, United Kingdom